HOSPITAL PRAYERS

*A Devotional for When Your Child Needs
Blessings & Bandaids*

SHANNON ALFORD

Hospital Prayers, *A Devotional for When Your Child Needs Blessings & Bandaids*

Author: Shannon Alford

Copyright 2019 Stars in the Sand Press

A special thank you to the following for their appreciated contributions to Hospital Prayers:

Guest Authors
Tina Cole
Meredith Adams

Editor
Amy Coffmon

Design Consultants
Shani Thornton
XO Studio

For my parents,
Bill and Sharon Dencer,
whose love and prayers
have blessed my life and so many others.

For my husband and daughter,
Ed and Audrey,
who inspire me every day
and fill my life with love and purpose.

Contents

God's Got It

One night, late into my career working as a Child Life Specialist at a large pediatric hospital, I had a clear and vivid dream that felt more like an actual experience than it did a typical dream. In this dream, I was standing in a hospital room holding a patient, an adorable baby boy named Grayson, who lay resting contently in my arms when an angel who faced me revealed himself, a Being bathed in beautiful soft bright light. The angel stepped back and lovingly smiled at me, and I understood that we had both been holding Grayson with our arms intertwined underneath him. I felt the presence of love, and I knew this wasn't the first time he had joined us during Grayson's long hospitalization. It was a moment of deep contentment that was suddenly interrupted by a baby's cry from down the hall. It was a familiar cry belonging to a baby girl with complex heart problems who could be difficult to console at times because of her distress.

I glanced out in the hallway in response to her cries, knowing I needed to transfer Grayson to his crib so I could go comfort her. I gazed back at the angel who spoke to me without words that "he's got it." He turned to leave, and I could visualize him walking down the hall to her room as her cries subsided and I sensed he was holding and rocking her.

Trust that God's "got it" with all of us. He loves our children, and he loves us, his children, with the consuming love of the Heavenly Father that he is.

Dear Lord,

You know me completely and all that concerns me. Help me to see you and know you in greater ways for you watch over me and delight in me. Quiet my anxious heart with your love. Help me remember that you rejoice over me with singing for I am yours.

In Jesus' name,
Amen

For he will command his angels concerning you to guard you in all your ways; they will lift you up in their hands, so that you will not strike your foot against a stone.

Psalm 91:11–12

The LORD your God is with you, he is mighty to save. He will take great delight in you, he will quiet you with his love, he will rejoice over you with singing.

Zephaniah 3:17

Emergency Prayers

My Child Life career began many years ago when I was hired by our local Children's Hospital to implement the first Child Life program in their busy ER (Emergency Room), also commonly referred to as the ED (Emergency Department).

What an intimidating and intense place to work. I had little guidance, so I learned as I went and was exposed to a great many situations, personalities, skill sets, and dynamics. It was a time of great learning and growth, both personally and professionally. I had never worked in a hospital before, and the ER had never had a Certified Child Life Specialist (CCLS) before. It's an environment that necessitates that connections form quickly, both between the patient, families, and staff as well as among individual staff members themselves which work collaboratively as part of a multidisciplinary team. Critical, traumatic, and demanding situations ebb and flow throughout the ER both day and night, exposing the fragility of life and emphasizing the common thread of humanity between us all.

It was during this high-intensity time in the early ER days working a typical evening shift when I heard my sister's voice call my name. I turned to find her holding my two-year-old nephew who was weak and frail in her arms. A nurse escorted them to a critical care room, and I followed. Drew had been ill and under a doctor's care when he became worse and was directed to the ER for work-up and evaluation.

After a difficult ER experience, Drew was admitted to the PICU (Pediatric Intensive Care Unit) with the diagnosis of meningitis and encephalitis where he was listed in critical condition, and we were advised his outcome was uncertain.

Those were very hard days. I experienced a level of fear, uncertainty, and sadness that was unfamiliar to me. I was a mess. During and following Drew's hospitalization, I questioned if Child Life was the right profession for me and if I had been mistaken about my aspirations. I also questioned what I knew or thought I knew about God, prayer, and faith.

But during that time when my world was shaken, my sister Amy had a quiet confidence about her. She was exhausted and overwhelmed, and Drew was clearly suffering greatly. Yet in addition to the sadness, Amy had a steadiness about her I couldn't describe or understand. My sister had a level of faith that was foreign to me even though we were raised in the same loving Christian home.

Amy prayed and interceded on Drew's behalf. She kept her Bible and notebook at her side and prayed scripture verses, proclaiming her little boy healed and restored in the name of Jesus. Drew's treatment and recovery progressed over time, and it was with hopeful and grateful hearts that our prayers were answered and my nephew was healed. This crisis was not the only one we have encountered as a family but it dramatically affected each of us in our varying levels of faith and belief.

My sister later told me she felt her hospital bedside prayers went straight from her lips to God's ears. During those dark days, Amy knew she wasn't alone. She felt the comfort and presence of the Lord, and she felt heard and understood, even in the midst of her grief.

Hospital prayers are emergency prayers. A child can be at the hospital for any number of reasons, but they all need prayer. There is a vulnerability when a child isn't well, and it is always concerning when a child doesn't look or act as they typically do.

Many prayers are prayed in hospitals, and they are often urgent passionate prayers. Hospital prayers are high-intensity prayers and often time-critical, as well, since circumstances and outcomes can change rapidly and unpredictably.

Now, all these years later, I am no stranger to emergency bedside prayers and the strength and comfort they bring. Working in the ER and on cardiology units for so many years has changed all that and so has becoming a wife and mother. Emergency prayers and all prayers go straight from our lips to God's ears. Prayer opens up the dialogue between heaven and earth and invites the presence of the living and loving God into our circumstances, our hearts, and our lives.

Dear Lord,

I call to you and pray for the life of my child and for my family. You alone are above my circumstances, and your wisdom and love exceed my distress and uncertainty. Act mightily on my behalf and reveal great and mighty things that only your revelation can reveal. Strengthen me in this moment for you are my Lord and my help.

In Jesus' name,
Amen

Pour out your heart like water in the presence of the Lord. Lift up your hands to him for the lives of your children.
> Lamentations 2:19

Call to me and I will answer you and tell you great and unsearchable things you do not know.
> Jeremiah 33:3

The Great Physician

"Is it going to hurt?" is a common question at a children's hospital. The truth is, a lot of things hurt. Boo boo's and heartaches and opposition and struggles.

Problems concerning health issues are particularly distressing, especially when it is regarding your child. When medical concerns arise, the best thing to do is to seek appropriate medical care and to call the Great Physician, who is the Lord.

The Bible contains much scripture and many accounts of health and healing within its pages. Exodus 15:26 says, "I am the LORD, who heals you." The Lord's healing exceeds physical healing alone. Psalm 103 instructs us to praise the Lord for forgiveness from all our sins and healing from all of our diseases, as well as other benefits.

John 4:47–53 gives an account of a government official who traveled to find Jesus and then begged him to heal his son, who was at home in another town, sick and close to death. After the official asked Jesus to come to his home to heal his child, Jesus told him, "You may go. Your son will live."

The government official believed the words of Jesus, and while he was still traveling back home, his servants met him with the news that his son was living. The boy's fever had left him at the precise time Jesus spoke the words that he would live. Jesus sent his word and healed him, which is exactly what Psalm 107:20 also says. The verse continues, "he rescued them from the grave."

In reading through some of the healing scriptures, I noticed a connection in some verses between healing and praising God. I think praising God keeps us close to him and his provision of peace, and helps guard us from fear.

Faith moves us forward, but fear pulls us back. Psalm 34:4 says, "I sought the LORD, and he answered me; he delivered me from all my fears." Health worries can escalate fear in the natural, but our God is supernatural and offers benefits which are the same. God can deliver us from sickness, sin, fear, or anything else. Nothing is too hard for him. Like the government official, we need to seek Jesus and believe his word. We're not to limit our understanding to only what we can see.

Jeremiah 33:6 says, "Nevertheless, I will bring health and healing to it; I will heal my people and will let them enjoy abundant peace and security." The Lord who heals and the Lord who saves is the one I will trust and praise, and I hope you do the same.

A favorite healing verse of mine is 2 Kings 20:5 which says, "I have heard your prayer and seen your tears; I will heal you." Another is Psalm 118:17, "I shall not die, but live, and declare the works of the LORD." Sometimes I write down a verse or two on index cards and place it in a visible place. My thoughts can quickly spiral downward if not kept in check with the truth of God's Word. Just find whatever works for you.

Each of us has a relationship with the Lord that is growing and changing and doesn't look like anyone else's. He knows the number of hairs on our head, and he gave us fingerprints that belong to us alone. So, let's live never forgetting all his benefits.

Dear Lord,

You crown me with your love and compassion and I praise you.

In Jesus' name,
Amen

Heal me, O LORD, and I will be healed; save me and I will be saved, for you are the one I praise.
Jeremiah 17:14

Praise the LORD, O my soul, and forget not all his benefits— who forgives all your sins and heals all your diseases, who redeems your life from the pit and crowns you with love and compassion, who satisfies your desires with good things so that your youth is renewed like the eagles.
Psalm 103:2–5

-4-

Because

As I was writing *Hospital Prayers*, it occurred to me that maybe some people would wonder why I wanted to write a devotional for the small and specific audience that I chose, which is for parents of hospitalized children. And the answer is: Because.

The answer is because as a Child Life Specialist, I have known and worked with many children and families in every type of situation, from the emergency department to intensive care. I have seen courage and faith in the lives of exhausted and stressed parents as they love, encourage, and care for their ill or hurt child, as well as tending to their family and to others around them.

I wanted to write this devotional because I see a need for one. All parents need to be reminded that God is in control, especially when threatening conditions arise and things feel out of control.

Every hospital has a culture all its own. It's a different place from the outside world, kind of

17

like an alternate reality. Big moments happen in hospitals. Pivotal moments, life and death moments, all are taking place in emergency rooms and patient rooms. Individually, each has a personal and powerful hospital experience that belongs to them alone, whether from the perspective of that as a patient, family, hospital worker, or other.

My work as a Child Life Specialist placed me in the unique position of meeting parents as they encountered stressful circumstances concerning their child. A parent described child life specialists as medical professionals who voluntarily entered into their world of pain, uncertainty, and confusion while providing support and comfort throughout.

Connections form quickly when you're meeting over a hurt or sick child. Frequent and extended hospitalizations develop those relationships further, with both patient and family. Child life specialists help children before, during, and after medical procedures and intervention. Child life specialists see the laughter and the tears, the playing and pain, the good days and the bad. Assessment and advocacy are ongoing throughout the hospitalization. It's not a typical relationship.

Child life specialists focus on a patient's development and coping as highest priorities, as well as working with the family of the child, whenever possible. Parents and hospital staff alike monitor medical progress and promote and assist in helping children reach developmental milestones, and positive coping, including play engagement.

During hospitalization, it's easy for parents to become emotionally fatigued and physically exhausted. Taking just a minute or two to pray or read scripture directs your mind on the Lord and gives perspective and strength that can't be achieved elsewhere.

This devotional is intentionally short in length and covers a variety of topics. Many of the devotions pertain to hospitalization, while others share biblical stories or personal accounts of God's presence in the moments of my daily life.

Some parents prefer to think and read about places and things outside the hospital, so I hope you find something within these pages that encourages you. Also, think about the people and places that bring you peace and joy and beauty and think beyond the hospital walls. Dream and hope about the days ahead, while finding the good in today, and pray for God's healing and clarity in guiding you.

Each devotional is followed by a prayer and scripture. Parents tend to pray for their children and spouses and everyone else, but often forget to pray for themselves. We all need prayer, and these prayers were written specifically for you.

I have found marriage and parenthood as avenues to great and ongoing personal and spiritual growth. These intimate and precious relationships increase our capacity to love a kazillion times beyond what we've known before and cultivates characteristics and skills not previously realized.

Parenthood is a blessing and a joy and a stressor. I wrote *Hospital Prayers* because I wanted to remind you, from one parent to another, that you are doing a good job. You're doing even better than you realize. God loves you. He is with you and for you. May God bless you and your family, both today and in the days to come.

Dear Lord,

Thank you that because you love me, you call me yours. Watch over my family. Heal us and save us through the power of Christ our Lord.

In Jesus' name,
Amen

You will be blessed in the city and blessed in the country. The fruit of your womb will be blessed, and the crops of your land and the young of your livestock—the calves of your herds and the lambs of your flocks.

Deuteronomy 28:3–4

She speaks with wisdom, and faithful instruction is on her tongue. She watches over the affairs of her household and does not eat the bread of idleness. Her children arise and call her blessed; her husband also, and he praises her.

Proverbs 31:26–28

5

Breathe

Many people hold their breath during times of stress. This affects the oxygen supply to the brain and body, making it difficult to think or respond clearly. One of the ways that child life specialists help children manage the stress of hospitalization and medical procedures is by helping them use the power of their breath to calm their anxious minds and bodies.

Coping tools are used, such as pinwheels or bubbles, for assistance in focus on breathing. When no props are available, strategies are used such as singing or pretending to blow out birthday candles on an imaginary cake.

Crying babies with heart conditions can dangerously elevate their heart rate, so much attention and assistance is given to calm and soothe them to help them regulate their breathing for their emotional and physical well-being.

Genesis 2:7 describes the first breath of life. It says, "The LORD God formed the man from the dust of the ground and breathed into his nostrils the breath of life, and the man became a living being." Scripture is referred to as God-breathed in 2 Timothy 4:16 and describes it as useful for teaching and equipping the people of God for good works.

The quality of your breathing greatly influences your physical well-being and state of mind. I recall one particularly stressful day at work and seeing a coworker I only occasionally saw in passing. She was a yoga therapist, and we paused for a minute to talk. She could clearly see I did not have a light-hearted demeanor and she invited me into a conference room for some deep-breathing exercises.

Right away, the heaviness of the stress which was restricting my breathing began to subside and was replaced by waves of relief. Just as I began to notice the depth of the paint color on the wall, my friend advised me I would notice a color difference on the wall because eyes require a lot of oxygen. With her guidance, in a very short amount of time, I felt calm and focused, and I had a much better rest of the day.

Everybody knows that regular exercise and an active lifestyle affects the quality of comprehensive health and the quality of life. In recent years, I had to overcome my perception of regular, consistent exercise as the equivalent to extreme sports. Our God can restore health and focus and purpose and restoration has been evident in my life.

Exercise classes have improved my health and wellness, but the focus on the breath work has been transforming. As a child life specialist, I helped others focus on their breathing, and in Barre3, I have learned to pay greater attention to mine.

My teacher Jane says to breathe in the good and blow out the bad. She says it all begins with the breath. Focusing on my breath and focusing on good has helped me develop a greater awareness of myself and a greater awareness of the Spirit of God who has made me. "Let everything that has breath praise the LORD," says Psalm 150:6.

Dear Lord,

I praise You for your breath gives life.

In Jesus' name,
Amen

Then the LORD God formed the man from the dust of the ground and breathed into his nostrils the breath of life, and the man became a living being.
Genesis 2:7

The Spirit of God has made me, and the breath of the Almighty gives me life.
Job 33:4

6

Play Time

A nurse I talked to one day told me she likes working with children because although it is challenging, it is also rewarding. After her nursing clinicals, she chose pediatrics over adult care because she said that the adults complain all day, but the children play.

Play is the language of children and play is essential to their physical and emotional development and well-being. Play is sequential and is important to healthy brain development.

Child life specialists use different types of play opportunities and interventions in working with children to help reduce anxiety and promote positive coping and adjustment. Medical play is used to teach about a diagnosis or procedure and offers children the opportunity to interact with the medical equipment and supplies to gain understanding and mastery. Therapeutic play addresses specific issues or goals, such as promoting play activities which encourage mobility and movement after surgery.

Developmental play is used for normalization and to promote typical development.

We want kids playing because interest in play signals interest in life. For the child too young or sick to play, adaptaions are made. Crib mobiles, soothing music, and books provide calming developmental support, and quieter types of play are used for short amounts of time. Child life specialists tailor play inventions to accommodate each child and situation.

I remember a parent asking me, "You know what a really big deal this is, don't you?" as I held her three-year-old daughter's hand in mine while pushing her I.V. (intravenous hydration) with the other. We had been leaving her patient room to walk to the playroom for the first time after she had been on bedrest in intensive care for an extended time. It was a special day and one we had worked towards for a long time.

But the thing is, it really is a big deal to play. We can learn a lot by observing children and dogs. Children leave play differently than they began it. Some play is fun play and some play is serious, but it all accomplishes something in the process.

We all need margin in our life for play. 3 John 1:1 says, "Dear friend, I pray that you may enjoy good health and that all may go well with you, even as your soul is getting along well." I think play is needed for our soul to prosper. It seems to me that in play, much like prayer, that it is through the process of engagement that transformation takes place.

Play can also help us cope with sadness and overcome fear. This is often seen in the playroom. One example is a preschooler I worked with who was in heart failure. He began to regress developmentally and emotionally throughout his extended hospitalization. Meanwhile, his fear and anxiety escalated. He became afraid to leave his room because it usually meant he was taken for a procedure somewhere in the hospital, but his mom insisted child life interventions occur in the nearby playroom because he always came back happy, even when he didn't want to go.

Positive changes began to occur throughout those playroom activities. The once fearful child soon gained confidence, his developmental regression ended, and he appeared much happier and outgoing.

One day in the playroom, he told me that we were dinosaurs and he basically described how we were going to destroy the city. We built towers out of blocks and then roared and stomped while knocking them down. Through the power of play, his behavior and attitude reflected a change in his adjustment to the scary situation of a heart transplant, which he came through successfully.

Proverbs 17:22 says, "A cheerful heart is good medicine, but a crushed spirit dries up the bones." Jesus says, "Come to me, all you who are weary and burdened, and I will give you rest." At the hospital, play is good medicine. It helps those who are cheerful and those who are weary.

Among other names, children have called me "the art doctor." And this art doctor prescribes that you take time to play and time to pray so that all may go well with you.

Dear Lord,

You have given us children as a blessing and a gift. Thank you for the blessing of being a parent. May we have childlike faith to follow you.

In Jesus' name,
Amen

Jesus said, "Let the little children come to me, and do not hinder them, for the kingdom of God belongs to such as these.

Mark 10:14

A cheerful heart is good medicine, but a crushed spirit dries up the bones.

Proverbs 17:22

7

The Best Day Ever

Inspiration often comes from unexpected places. Between my roles as mom and child life specialist, I've probably watched more episodes of SpongeBob SquarePants than the typical adult. And quite honestly, I like his attitude.

Although SpongeBob SquarePants is a cartoon character, he demonstrates some admirable qualities such as a positive attitude, kindness, contentment, loyalty, and a work ethic. SpongeBob lives in a pineapple under the sea with his pet sea snail Gary and lives peacefully in his community.

Like everyone, SpongeBob sometimes encounters adversity. Yet he displays love and concern for others, appreciating different personalities and encouraging respect and cooperation.

Songs and music are used throughout the show to convey messages, and SpongeBob sings about such things as a typical day being the best day ever, having fun and an attitude of gratitude. And

35

if that wasn't already enough for a cartoon character, SpongeBob is also an expert bubble blower with his own specific technique, and I can appreciate that.

Bubbles are frequently given out and used in the hospital. Not only are bubbles fun and interesting to many age groups, but they also have therapeutic value in the medical setting. Bubbles can be used as a distraction strategy to help children calm their minds and bodies to focus their attention in a positive way during stressful moments.

Blowing bubbles encourage deep breathing for relaxation and help clear the lungs to reduce the risk of breathing problems such as pneumonia after surgery. Children enjoy popping bubbles, and it can empower them and give them a sense of choice and control, especially in a situation where they don't have much control.

Many of my co-workers were also well-versed in all things SpongeBob as well as other cultural influences on the population we serve. The silliness of the show has a wide appeal and humor is always a great point of connection between people. Humor helps diffuse anxiety and stress and fosters a collaborative approach to interacting.

Hospitalization places unique demands on people. Being in an intimidating and unfamiliar setting full of new sights and sounds and strangers, all while not feeling well would be overwhelming to anyone. It's an out-of-the-ordinary experience, in a strange new community, with adversity to overcome.

Like the many children who have made an impression on me, SpongeBob reminds me to find the silly, even in the serious; to find laughter, even among the tears; and to embrace individuality while engaging in the connection of community. It's the little things that are the big things: blowing bubbles, making friends, being thankful and finding good every day.

Dear Lord,

This is the best day ever
because you have made it.

In Jesus' name,
Amen

A cheerful heart is good medicine, but a crushed spirit dries up the bones.

Proverbs 17:22

This is the day that the LORD has made; let us rejoice and be glad in it.

Psalm 118:24 (ESV)

8

Wisdom Calls

Navigating a health crisis is taxing in many ways. In addition to the emotional and physical toll of a diagnosis and all that follows, resources such as time, energy and finances are impacted. There are other areas also affected such as relationships, employment, schedules, and other obligations.

I once had an experience where while facing a health crisis and treatment path, I visited various specialists for evaluation and treatment. At each appointment, everything just felt wrong from deep inside, as though I didn't belong there. My husband sensed the same, but we tried to figure out if we were upset about the illness in general or concerned about the treatment and outcomes or if we were hesitant about the medical providers themselves.

I confided in some friends and asked for their advice, including a friend who urged me to come over and talk to her husband. He had undergone extensive medical care and was full of good advice. He told me about a negative experience he had before he changed doctors and he recommended I get a second opinion before I proceed with anything.

The next day I emailed a friend who had an affiliation with another medical facility. She responded with a recommendation for a physician, as well as soothing words of encouragement.

Our meeting with the new physician was in stark contrast to what we had experienced with the first. This doctor came into the room with a calm demeanor, and our interaction conveyed her expertise and interest. She explained things clearly, asked and answered questions, provided options available and shared her recommendations while asking for my opinion. By the end of the visit, although I still didn't like the diagnosis, I had the assurance that I was in the care of capable hands. That appointment completely changed the course of my treatment and included beneficial holistic therapies and care.

This new doctor was compassionate. She managed to convey an understanding of the difficulty facing illness while encouraging me in full recovery. A second doctor at another appointment told me I was young and would live a long life. While I know not every doctor can or would make that statement to a patient, I sensed they were speaking life and not death over me as Proverbs 18:21 describes. I know my Lord can speak through anyone or anything and he speaks specifically to situations.

My doctor also agreed that we should proceed with our scheduled vacation for a planned break to think about things before starting treatment.

That short break helped me to recover a little bit emotionally as well as shift me mentally to prepare for the battle ahead. I always knew in my heart that victory was in store, but I also knew from the past that I needed strength and wisdom that only comes through the supernatural realm of the Lord. I benefited from some quiet time with the Commander in Chief before I headed into battle and I left that battle victorious.

One of my favorite verses is Nehemiah 7:5 which begins with, "So my God put it into my heart." There have been many times where initially I've been confused about a situation and haven't known what to do. What I eventually learned is that continued thought and prayer will lead to clarity, asking God for wisdom, understanding, and guidance.

I've found that often after indecision, answers arrive swiftly and firmly. Suddenly I will have answers that I didn't have previously, like God simply put them into my heart.

God willingly gives wisdom if we ask him for it. James 1:5 says, "If any of you lacks wisdom, you should ask God, who gives generously to all without finding fault, and it will be given to you."

King Solomon was a king of Israel revered for his wisdom and wealth. 2 Chronicles 1 documents how the Lord his God was with him and made him exceedingly great. One night God appeared to Solomon and said to him, "Ask for whatever you want me to give you." Solomon answered by asking for wisdom and knowledge to lead the people God had given him responsibility for. God rewarded him not only with wisdom and knowledge but also gave him wealth, riches and honor.

Wisdom calls us from our current place and leads us forward. Statistics and clinical trials didn't matter in my recoveries. What mattered was wisdom and knowing the wisdom I was receiving was from the Lord, whose wisdom exceeds all understanding.

Decisions determine outcomes and outcomes can be the difference between life and death. The Giver of Life is also the Giver of Wisdom, and he calls wisdom a good thing and a preserver of life.

Dear Lord,

You are a God of wisdom and you are my shelter. Protect me and guide me with knowledge of your ways and preserve my life. Guide me in all understanding so I may fulfill the call you have on my life and walk in the fullness of all you have for me.

In Jesus' name,
Amen

Wisdom, like an inheritance, is a good thing and benefits those who see the sun. Wisdom is a shelter as money is a shelter, but the advantage of knowledge is this: that wisdom preserves the life of its possessor.
Ecclesiastes 7:11–12

So then my God put it into my heart.
Nehemiah 7:5

9

Shine

I've known many wonderful parents, including foster and adoptive parents. One foster mom I met in the ER told me, "All children are ours" and talked about how children need positive role models and interactions to foster their well-being. Her philosophy reflects the attitude of teamwork and collaboration between the patient, family, and staff at the hospital. Another adoptive parent I met shared a verse she found especially meaningful, Matthew 5:16, "let your light shine before men, that they may see your good deeds and praise your Father in heaven."

As we work together in the physical realm, God has appointed angels to protect his children in the spiritual realm. 1 Corinthians 15:44 says, "If there is a natural body, there is also a spiritual body." Matthew 18:10 refers to children's angelic protection which says, "See that you do not look down on one of these little ones. For I tell you that their angels in heaven always see the face of my Father in heaven."

Medical play is a type of play frequently used by child life specialists. Medical play provides children the opportunity to utilize real and play medical equipment using dolls or stuffed animals for fun, learning, and expression of feelings. During medical play with a ten-year-old, she told me about her arrival at the hospital. She had been swimming with her brother at the community pool before passing out in the water. She told me she saw God, golden gates and angels before suddenly waking up in the ER. She also explained to me that angels come in all sizes, like people. She didn't remember anything that happened between heaven and the hospital including her medical flight to the hospital. She had been unresponsive before being resuscitated.

After being admitted to intensive care for several days, she was transferred to the cardiology unit. Both family and staff realized her recovery for the miracle that it was. She had been in the presence of our Holy God, and her peace and joy were evident.

The angels, like us, are created by God and under his sovereign reign. Psalm 91:11 says, "For he will command his angels concerning you to guard you in all your ways."

In John 8:12, Jesus said, "I am the light of the world. Whoever follows me will never walk in darkness, but will have the light of life." Light was created in Genesis 1:3 when God said, "Let there be light."

God extends his light to us and through us. When we follow him, we don't walk in darkness but instead, are a reflection of his light which guides us and shows the world we are his.

It reminds me of the Sunday school song, "This little light of mine, I'm going to let it shine." There is powerful truth in the message of this little song. It makes me think of the candlelight service at church on Christmas Eve. Near the end of the service, the lights are dimmed, and the candles are lit while the congregation sings "Silent Night, Holy Night."

There are holy moments within everyday moments. Find the good within the bad, see the miracles revealed in the ordinary and let's encourage each other to let our little light shine.

Dear Lord,

Thank you for sending your son Jesus as the light of the world and for your angelic protection. May I praise you with my life and reflect that I am yours.

In Jesus' name,
Amen

You are the light of the world. A city on a hill cannot be hidden. Neither do people light a lamp and put it under a bowl. Instead they put it on its stand, and it gives light to everyone in the house.

In the same way, let your light shine before men, that they may see your good deeds and praise your Father in heaven.
Matthew 5: 14–16

See that you do not look down on one of these little ones. For I tell you that their angels in heaven always see the face of my Father in heaven.
Matthew 18:10

10

Joking

My best friend's last name is King. She and I have a love and understanding of one another that is similar to sisterhood. She lives in town, but we really don't talk very often because the dynamics of friendships change during different seasons of life, but not the depth.

When I went through a health crisis, she told me that the winds of opposition coming against me were the same winds that would change direction to be at my back to propel me forward.

When I later faced another, she told me I was equipped for the battle and reminded me of past victories while showering me with gifts and words of encouragement.

During various times of distress, she reminded me that problems, though difficult, were opportunities to trust God in a greater way.

We met through my husband when he and I were still dating. They were a family of five. She once told me she couldn't name either of her sons after her father whose name is Joseph because she didn't want him to have to say, "Hi, I'm Joe King" which sounds like, "Hi, I'm joking." Moms think about these things.

Our friends became first-time grandparents this year. Their granddaughter was born with a serious medical problem detected in the hospital after her birth. She was transferred to a NICU (Neonatal Intensive Care Unit) at children's hospital where she was hospitalized for several months.

In the close quarters of NICU, they learned there were two babies with the last name King. The other baby was a boy. His name was Joe. And she wasn't joking.

She was concerned that Joe never had any visitors and he was always alone except for the medical staff that cared for him. She had asked the staff if they could sit at his bedside though they weren't surprised that hospital policy prohibited that.

I told her there are lots of reasons why families don't visit their children and many of the children who are hospitalized live out of town or even further away than that. Some children are hospitalized frequently or for extended periods.

Not all families can provide the optimal level of care and support to their children physically or emotionally. Some don't have the resources or flexibility to do so, and others don't have the capacity. Sometimes children are in foster care and some are born in jail. Many people love their children but have limitations beyond our understanding. The hospital has staff and resources to assist families but what we can do on a personal level is pray.

The Kings are a family of prayer. They are a big family and have lots of friends. Many people prayed for the hospitalized King babies. Baby girl came home and is doing great. We don't know how baby boy is doing but another name for Jesus Christ in 1 Peter 6:15 is the King of kings and the Lord of lords, and he knows Joe King's outcome. And that's good enough for me.

Sometimes we are prompted to pray for others, and sometimes others are prompted to pray for us. God uses the willing for his purposes. And that's no joke.

Dear Lord,

You are the King of kings and Lord of lords who sees and knows everything. Thank you, God, that you do not allow the waters to overtake me as I pass through them because you have summoned me by name and I am yours.

In Jesus' name,
Amen

Do not fear, for I have redeemed you; I have summoned you by name; you are mine. When you pass through the waters, I will be with you; and when you pass through the rivers, they will not sweep over you. When you walk through the fire, you will not be burned; the flames will not set you ablaze. For I am the LORD your God, the Holy One of Israel, your Savior.
     Isaiah 43:1–3a

Is anyone of you in trouble? Let them pray. Is anyone happy? Let them sing songs of praise. Is anyone among you sick? Let them call the elders of the church to pray over them and anoint them with oil in the name of the Lord. And the prayer offered in faith will make the sick person well; the Lord will raise them up. If he has sinned, he will be forgiven. Therefore confess your sins to each other and pray for each other so that you may be healed. The prayer of a righteous person is powerful and effective.

James 5:13–16

-11-
Character Traits

The book of Proverbs is a book of the wisdom of God. It gives insight and instruction on how to live a peaceful and happy life with many of the verses pertaining to our character in daily living.

Proverbs 11:3 says, "The integrity of the upright guides them." Character refinement is soul work and sanctification is one of God's specialties. We were born sinful in a fallen world surrounded by temptation, but the Lord guides us in paths of loving correction and uprightness as he shapes who we are to become more a reflection of who he is.

Character is important to God and also important to the fulfillment of our life's purpose which is to love God and love others. Ephesians 4 urges us to live a life worthy of the calling we have received through the Lord who is over all and through all and in all. The chapter ends with the following instruction, "Be kind and compassionate to one another, forgiving one another, just as in Christ God forgave you."

Refinement occurs when we are open to seeking and receiving the Lord's revelation and direction. Proverbs 9:9 says, "Instruct a wise man and he will be wiser still." It is explained in Proverbs 10:8 that those who receive the Lord's commands walk on secure paths. The verse also mentions consequences for those who choose crooked paths, so there is a direct correlation between a person's character, the decisions they make and the outcome of their choices. Our legacy is linked to our character.

Proverbs 29:6 says, "An evil man is snared by his own sin, but a righteous one can sing and be glad." The quality of life is much better when you can sing and be glad instead of being ensnared by sin. God wants us to enjoy our life and a cheerful heart is referred to as good medicine in Proverbs 17:22. Our heart is cheerful because our hope and faith is in God and not in ourselves or our circumstances.

Ephesians 3:20 tells us that God is able to do immeasurably more than all we ask or imagine, according to his power that is at work within us. He changes us from the inside out not only for our benefit but to also impact the world around us for good.

The difficult times of adversity are never easy but often going through hard situations produces significant personal growth that leads to advancement or new beginnings. God never wastes our pain, and he uses all things for our good including the process of affliction for accomplishing something bigger than we can see.

We are to live a lifestyle aware of the limitless possibilities of God. As we encounter various people or phases in life, some of which we like and some of which we don't, maybe they can be used for our good if we are receptive to growing in faith and perspective.

My friend Dwayne has mentioned the spiritual significance of the work we do in the ER. A hospital chaplain called our children's hospital "holy grounds." Sacred moments happen all the time with God in our midst. Through our work, we serve others, and I think through the act of serving, we discover and develop our gifts. When our hands are open to giving, our hands are also open to receiving. We receive life, prosperity, and honor and these are found by those who pursue righteousness and love as written in Proverbs 21:21. All who pursue it will find it.

God sees potential we can't perceive. May we be wise in heart to accept commands so that we are people of integrity who walk securely. Let's partner with the God of the universe and say "yes" to potential that is immeasurably more than all we ask or imagine.

Dear Lord,

Help my heart accept your commands
and guide me in your wisdom and uprightness.

In Jesus' name,
Amen

The wise in heart accept commands, but a chattering fool comes to ruin. The man of integrity walks securely, but he who takes crooked paths will be found out.
        Proverbs 10:8–9

Now to him who is able to do immeasurably more than all we ask or imagine, according to his power that is at work within us, to him be glory in the church and in Christ Jesus throughout all generations, for ever and ever! Amen.

Ephesians 3:20

-12-

Donkey

You may know about the lovable and talking donkey from the movie Shrek but did you know there's a story about a talking donkey in the Bible?

My vague recollection was that some man beat his donkey and the donkey was given the ability to talk so he had a chat with his owner about it. The man was so angry he argued back before he realized he was arguing with an animal. I decided to search and read about it again and found the account in the Old Testament book of Numbers in chapter 22.

It's a really interesting story about a man named Balaam. I encourage you to read it for yourself, but a brief synopsis is that Balaam was a spiritual leader who could invoke blessing or curses over people and it would come to pass. He was summoned by the king of Moab to curse the Israelites. Balaam asked God about it, and God said to Balaam in Numbers 22:12, "Do not go with them. You must not put a curse on those people, because they are blessed."

Balaam understood God's answer but was tempted by the promise of the king's reward, so he saddled his donkey and began the journey to see the king, accompanied by princes the king had sent to summon him.

Three times Balaam's donkey veered off the path, and each time Balaam beat the poor donkey with his staff. What Balaam didn't realize was his donkey had saved his life each time she turned off the road because there was an angel of the LORD with a drawn sword in his hand that stood before them.

A conversation between Balaam and his donkey ensues beginning in Numbers 22:28–29 when the Lord opened the donkey's mouth, and she said to Balaam, "What have I done to you to make you beat me these three times?"

Balaam answered the donkey, "You have made a fool of me! If I had a sword in my hand, I would kill you now." The Lord opened Balaam's eyes in verse 31, and he saw the angel of the LORD standing in the road with his sword drawn.

Balaam responded by bowing low and fell facedown before the angel of the LORD. Then the angel of the LORD asked Balaam why he had beaten his donkey three times and told him he had come to oppose him.

There's a lot of content contained in these scriptures to consider, but I'm pondering the donkey. She was in physical and emotional pain from her owner's cruelty and abuse. Numbers 29:30 documents the donkey asking Balaam, "Am I not your own donkey, which you have always ridden, to this day? Have I been in the habit of doing this to you?" Balaam answered, "No."

The words of the donkey clearly illustrate her distress. It's also interesting to note that the donkey knew how to count. She recounted that she was beaten and she was beaten not once or twice, but three times.

I wonder if the donkey appreciated that the angel of the LORD spoke on her behalf? The angel of the LORD asked Balaam directly why he had beaten his donkey three times, and the angel also informed him he would have killed Balaam but spared the donkey if Balaam had proceeded on his journey to meet the king of Moab.

Did the donkey wonder why the angel of the LORD waited so long before stepping in while Balaam unleashed his fury on her three times? Was she grateful to the angel of the LORD for planning to spare her life but not Balaam's if he had forced the donkey to continue?

I'm curious if the donkey experienced anger. With her newly given ability to speak, was she tempted to say words to Balaam that would curse and not bless? Like perhaps referring to him using another name for donkey?

Was the donkey able to forgive Balaam quickly? Among the negative, I also find positive aspects to this story. From the donkey's words, I get the impression she felt a sense of fulfillment that she had an owner and a purpose. They had a history together, and it doesn't appear like it included seeing an angel of the LORD with a drawn sword or getting beaten. They were having an unusual and bad day because of Balaam's disobedience to God. Balaam's sin affected his donkey and could have affected the people of Israel who were getting ready to go into the Promised Land.

What also impresses me is that the donkey was known by the Lord and didn't question it. The donkey questioned Balaam, and Balaam questioned the Lord, but the donkey didn't question God.

The Lord saw the donkey's reverence when seeing the angel of the LORD. He saw her anguish and knew her thoughts and responded by allowing her to speak. I think it's safe to assume that donkey also received comfort and healing from her holy encounter.

God loves and cares about his creation. If God cares that much about a donkey, how much more love and concern does he have for his people?

During my many years in Child Life, about half of the inpatient population of hospital beds were filled with infants. As the hospital continued to grow and more inpatient beds and NICU (Neonatal Intensive Care Unit) units were added, the need for those beds continued to grow as well.

God knows every single child in every single bed. Each is precious in his sight. Even the smallest and frailest of babies have the knowledge and understanding that God knows them and loves them. Jeremiah 1:5 says, "Before I formed you in the womb I knew you."

The greatest calling God has on our life is for us to know him. That is the greatest desire of his heart. And today my inspiration comes from a donkey.

Dear Lord,

Because you love me, you satisfy me with long life and show me your salvation. May my path never oppose you.

In Jesus' name,
Amen

The angel of the LORD asked him, "Why have you beaten your donkey these three times? I have come here to oppose you because your path is a reckless one before me. The donkey saw me and turned away from me these three times. If she had not turned away, I would certainly have killed you by now, but I would have spared her." Balaam said to the angel of the LORD, "I have sinned. I did not realize you were standing in the road to oppose me."

Numbers 22:32–34b

"Because he loves me," says the LORD, "I will rescue him; I will protect him, for he acknowledges my name. He will call upon me, and I will answer him; I will be with him in trouble, I will deliver him and honor him. With long life will I satisfy him and show him my salvation.

Psalm 91:14–16

-13-

An Unlikely Army

I'm part of a prayer group that meets weekly at my friend Susan's house to pray for the students and staff at the high school. The organization is called Moms in Prayer International, and its vision is that every school in the world would be prayed for.

We pray, talk, laugh and drink a lot of coffee. My friend Kathy calls us an "unlikely army." We refer to ourselves as the ninjas, short for prayer ninja warriors, which we prefer to the acronym MIP (moms in prayer). Actually, I'm pretty sure the name ninja was unofficially adopted after someone's son asked her if there was a Dads in Prayer because he wanted to be a DIP when he grew up.

We mamas know these are hard days for kids to grow up in and have prayed through bomb threats and lockdowns and all sorts of issues and situations. We've seen a lot of answered prayer. We recently learned that some teachers in our community have started meeting weekly before school to pray through their schools. We moms enjoy our time together. We have a sense of peace and security that our prayers make a difference. We also pray for kids who don't have anyone praying for them. Matthew 18:19 says, "Again, I tell you that if two of you on earth agree about anything you ask for, it will be done for you by my Father in heaven. For where two or three come together in my name, there am I with them." We are united in desiring God's best for each young life and that gives God more room to work when we ask for his help.

God delights in the presence and prayers of his people, but I imagine he especially enjoys the prayers of children. While going through old journals recently, I found a story about my nephew Nick when he was seven years old that my sister-in-law had told me. Their neighbors had many children and had encountered financial problems. One of the little girls told Nick she overheard her parents talking one day about how they only had ten dollars. She was really worried.

Nick suggested they pray about it and she agreed. He then led her to the trampoline in his back yard where they jumped up and down praying to God for help. Then Nick began to reach his hands to the sky every time he jumped up so he would be closer to God. My sister-in-law watched as they jumped and laughed and prayed. They, too, are an unlikely army, fighting in joy against the threat of darkness and inviting in God's great light and provision.

God answered their prayers for that family who successfully overcame that difficult time. The problems we encounter aren't meant to destroy us, but to strengthen us and build us up. Whether troubles happen to us or are the consequences of poor decisions, Romans 8:28 assures us that God works for our good in all things. Bad situations can be turned around and used in expected ways for our good.

Whether in a living room or on a trampoline, it is good to gather and laugh and play and pray. God can take the ordinary of children's play to perform the miraculous and thwart the plans of the enemy of our souls.

I can imagine what my sister-in-law saw watching Nick and his friend on the trampoline that day. I can also imagine the Lord answering them as they reached up to the sky. Isaiah 65:24 says, "Before they call I will answer; while they are still speaking I will hear." May all of God's people, the young and old alike, learn from each other and know that God is good.

Dear Lord,

Apart from you there is no Savior. When you act, no one can reverse it. Thank you that you answer me even before I call you. I am yours and I am blessed.

In Jesus' name,
Amen

He will bless those who fear the LORD— small and great alike. May the LORD cause you to flourish, both you and your children. May you be blessed by the LORD, the Maker of heaven and earth.

Psalm 115:13–15

"You are my witnesses," declares the LORD, "and my servant whom I have chosen so that you may know and believe me and understand that I am he. Before me no god was formed, nor will there be one after me. I, even I, am the LORD, and apart from me there is no savior. I have revealed and saved and proclaimed— I, and not some foreign god among you. You are my witnesses," declares the LORD, "that I am God. Yes, and from ancient days I am he. No one can deliver out of my hand. When I act, who can reverse it?"

Isaiah 43:10–13

Vineyard

A visiting pastor at my old church preached a sermon with a lasting and meaningful message. He spoke about vineyards. The Bible teaches many lessons and parables about vineyards. John 15 describes how God the Father is the gardener of the field tending to his vineyard, Jesus is the true vine and we are the branches. John 15:8 says, "This is to my Father's glory, that you bear much fruit, showing yourselves to be my disciples."

The pastor told us we will one day meet our Lord directly and he will ask us what we did with our vineyard. The pastor said we live in a fallen, broken world in overwhelming need but we are not to be discouraged because God has the whole world in his hands. We are not to despair, but we are encouraged to be good stewards in tending to our "vineyard," which is our scope of influence.

Our vineyard is made up of our family and friends, our community and workplace, and all of those we come in contact with. We are to love and give and help those around us while growing in God's wisdom and character as he uses people and circumstances to refine us so we may become more like him.

Isaiah 27:2–3 describes singing about a fruitful vineyard which the Lord watches over, watering it continually and guarding it day and night. Psalm 128:3 refers to a wife as a fruitful vine flourishing within the home with children like olive shoots around the table.

In contrast to a fruitful vineyard, a description of the field of a sluggard is portrayed in Proverbs 24:30–31. The ground is described as being covered with weeds and thorns with the stone wall in ruins around it. And the sluggard, which is clearly not a favorable term, is described as lacking judgment.

Jesus is referred to as the Lord of the harvest in Matthew 9:38. The prior verses describe Jesus having great compassion on the crowds of people following him as he went through towns and villages teaching about the Kingdom of God and healing every disease and illness. He saw the distressed and hurting people and compared them to sheep without a shepherd and referred to them as a field ripe for harvest. In Matthew 9:37–38, Jesus said to his disciples, "The harvest is plentiful but the workers are few. Ask the Lord of the harvest, therefore, to send out workers into his harvest field."

I can imagine the desperation of those needing physical and spiritual healing. Large crowds and long waits of sick and hurt children are not uncommon sights in the ER. Families arrive at the ER expecting to receive medical care. No one comes to sit in the waiting room for hours simply to return home without treatment nor would any hospital worker want a patient to leave the hospital without receiving the medical care they need.

In the ER, workers are used to bringing provision and help to patients and families. In the world, workers are used to accomplish God's will to reach the lost and bring in the Lord's harvest. Jesus had compassion on the crowds, he has compassion for us and it is with compassion we can share the transforming love of God with others. Jesus taught and preached and healed then, and he still does now. He used his disciples then and he does the same today.

We all have a vineyard. It's up to us how we tend to it and how we tend to it will determine if our fields produce fruit or thorns.

Dear Lord,

May you sing about the fruitful vineyard of my life, as you watch over me and guard me both day and night.

In Jesus' name,
Amen

I went past the field of the sluggard, past the vineyard of the man who has no sense; thorns had come up everywhere, and the ground was covered with weeds, and the stone wall was in ruins.
Proverbs 24:30–31

In that day— "Sing about a fruitful vineyard; I, the LORD, watch over it; I water it continually. I guard it day and night so that no one may harm it."
Isaiah 27:2–3

15

Tears as Prayers

Sometimes there are just seasons of sadness. It can be a personal loss or something bigger that affects a community or nation. There have been times where I've felt weighted down by a blanket of heaviness. National disasters and acts of violence affect far more than just those involved but have a rippling effect. Sometimes our grief is beyond words. I believe God sees our tears as prayers. God knows our every problem and Psalm 56:8 tells us he sees every tear. Our tears are precious to him. According to John 11:35, Jesus wept after his friend Lazarus died. He proceeded to raise him from the dead, but the depth of his emotions resulted in tears.

I remember an extremely difficult season in the CTICU (Cardiothoracic Intensive Care Unit) when there were several deaths and sad situations that stretched out over a long period of time. The somber mood could be felt throughout the intensive care unit, and discouragement lingered behind closed doors at our weekly psychosocial rounds. Staff commented on what an unusual and difficult time it was.

We met in the staff break room which had bulletin boards on the wall. One was covered with hospital information and postings and another displayed children's artwork and thank you notes from families. I noticed a photo of a former patient accompanied by a card with calling hours and the family's note of thanks for the care they received in the CTICU. Printed on the card was Psalm 139:16 which says, "All the days ordained for me were written in your book before one of them came to be."

People are amazing, especially when their faith shines through the brokenness and pain in their lives. After their loss, they formed a foundation in their son's honor, as have some other families I've known, and they are involved in several projects which benefit children and their families.

There were a lot of tears during that time. There are messages in tears and God knows the exact meaning behind each one. We see a lot of tears in the hospital, especially in the ER. I remember standing in a trauma room observing my first trauma, which resulted from a five-year-old boy getting hit by a car. He was brought to the ER by ambulance. The trauma nurse explained to me that the boy's crying was a good sign because it's a natural reaction to pain and fear. The kids they worry about are the kids that don't cry. The boy's dad arrived soon after he did and a short time later, x-rays revealed that he sustained only minimal injuries and that he would be fine.

As parents and hospital workers, we try to identify the reason for tears because pain and fear are addressed through different approaches. One day while working on the cardiology unit, I walked by a room where a two-year-old was sobbing big, wet tears while his dad sat at his bedside talking to him and trying to calm him. I visited another patient and afterward, stopped back at that room to introduce myself and assess child life needs. I mentioned I had seen the toddler crying when I previously walked by the room and how it was nice to see him content now.

The toddler's dad explained he and his wife had recently adopted his son from Africa and that they had a three-year-old son at home, too. The tears I had seen while walking by were tears for more chocolate cake. His son had never had cake before and loved it. It had come as dessert with his lunch, and his dad had intended to give him a few bites, but that was not agreeable to the toddler. The sleepy and contented little boy looking at me had a belly full of chocolate cake.

The book of Ecclesiastes was written by King Solomon. Ecclesiastes 3:1 says, "There is a time for everything, and a season for every activity under heaven." Ecclesiastes 3:4 continues, "a time to weep and a time to laugh, a time to mourn and a time to dance."

King Solomon said there is a time for everything, so I think maybe that also means there is a time to cry and a time to eat chocolate cake. Sometimes we need a little sweetness to go with the saltiness of our tears. This side of heaven, everything is mixed in together, the weeping and the laughing, the mourning and the dancing and the salty and the sweet.

Dear Lord,

You know when my heart aches. Ease my pain and strengthen me as only you can.

In Jesus' name,
Amen

My frame was not hidden from you when I was made in the secret place, when I was woven together in the depths of the earth, All the days ordained for me were written in your book before one of them came to be.

Psalm 139:15–16

My face is red with weeping, deep shadows ring my eyes.

Job 16:16

16

Capes and Caffeine

This summer I helped with VBS (vacation Bible school) and had a group of children starting kindergarten in the fall. The theme was the ever-popular superheroes, and through fun and interaction, lessons focused on having heart, courage, wisdom, hope, and strength.

Most of the kids returned wearing their capes every day, and some wore the paper masks all week they decorated on the first day. My group of superheroes consisted primarily of adorable and energetic little boys. Leaving very tired on day one, I assessed the need to increase my caffeine intake and volunteer support. I savored my increased coffee consumption each morning and recruited my nephew as a teen volunteer. Austin's a kid magnet, and for the remainder of the week, he had boys hanging on him, sitting next to him, following him or calling his name. I appreciated his help and enjoyed seeing all the interaction between them.

Parents shared how their children were having fun and were excited to come back each day. I enjoyed getting to know them and seeing little glimpses into their lives. One boy explained how instead of using a napkin, he sometimes likes to use his tongue to wipe his face. His explanation was followed by an impressive demonstration, even though we ultimately had to resort to a wet napkin after that particular snack. Regardless, the smile on his face was huge, with or without food on it.

Conversations centered around topics like the best and worst snacks, fun plans with Grandma, losing teeth, birthday parties and starting elementary school. Two of the kids confided in me about the loss of their dogs who had died and how they miss them. One of the kids had a bandage on her knee from a fall, and another child had serious food and seasonal allergies we had to keep an eye on. There were tears over one child's old and sick cat, and tears over another child's hurt feelings between two of the girls.

One day, one of the girls had to go "really bad" which sent us running down the hall holding hands to make it in time. Once we returned to the group and the discussion about John 6:9 of the boy who shared his small lunch with a huge

94

crowd, she asked why the boy had to share his food when Jesus is God and could just feed them by himself. It's a question we all ask. It took me a long time to realize that God works through us to love and serve in addressing matters that matter to him.

We talked a lot about loving your neighbor as yourself from Matthew 22:39 and our mission focus was feeding hungry people in India. We collected change all week, weighing it each day. We looked at the globe to see how far away India is from our home and talked about how God loves all the children of the world.

On the last day, we had special visitors—two Newfoundland service dogs. The owners, a retired SWAT officer and his wife, talked about some of the places the dogs visit to help people. They explained how the older dog taught the younger dog and how the dogs like to stay close together, having physical contact between them. Then the dog's owners invited the children to pet them and assured them that although they are big, they are also gentle and wouldn't hurt them.

Most of the kids were excited about the dogs. I was too. Some of the kids knew the dogs from previous visits to their preschool or library, but one boy hid behind me as we entered the room, saying he was afraid of dogs. He was very serious as he studied the situation and asked me questions. Finally, he stepped forward, and he briefly touched one of the dogs. Satisfied, he stepped back and looked at me. The look of fear was no longer on his face; his courage had strengthened him. His fear was real, but he didn't let it stop him from moving forward anyway. I witnessed his courage in action and was reminded once again that God is bigger than our fears. He leads us very specifically. While most the other kids were happily enjoying the dogs, this child was doing important work in moving through fear and practicing courage. Fear is personal and must be confronted individually. Each superhero wears his or her own cape and faces his or her own "bad guy" of fear, opposition or adversity.

Life isn't easy for any of us. Loss, allergies, sharing, and fears are just some of the many hard things we face, and they're hard things at any age. But when the awareness of God's love permeates our life, it changes us. We get braver and stronger when our faith is tested and when we experience firsthand how the joy of the Lord can be our strength.

Joy can't be contained; it starts on the inside and radiates outward. The best part of VBS was seeing all those kids singing, dancing, leaping, and striking their favorite superhero poses. Their capes moved as they grooved and I imagined our God's deep laughter of delight and the twinkle in his eyes as he watched upon the scene before him, his precious ones worshipping and singing songs of victory.

Dear Lord,

You teach the young and old alike that we should love our neighbor as we love ourself and to share what we have with others including the truth that your joy is strength and your favor is a shield. I sing songs of victory because my trust and faith is in you, both now and to infinity and beyond.

In Jesus' name,
Amen

For the LORD takes delight in his people.
Psalm 149:4

The joy of the LORD is your strength.
Nehemiah 8:10

-17-

Comfort

There are many challenges we encounter in which we must travail through. Having a child in the hospital or experiencing health issues can range from stressful to life-altering. It is a deeply personal and difficult journey, even when you are surrounded by love, support, and excellent medical care. My friend Meredith refers to it as "the heroic journey."

Hospitalization and medical procedures expose you to observations and experiences you couldn't have imagined and broadly expand your view. Having a sick or hurting child occupies your mind and heart and emotions.

Naturally, children are best comforted by the people they love, and mothers have a special way of consoling their child because of the relationship between them. The prophet Isaiah references this as well as illustrates that God comforts us. Isaiah 66:13 says, "As a mother comforts her child, so I will comfort you."

The greatest comfort to an aching mother's heart is the power and presence of God's unfailing love. In Matthew 5:4, Jesus refers to those who mourn as blessed because they will be comforted. Psalm 34:18 says the LORD is close to the brokenhearted and he saves those who are crushed in spirit. Just as we are drawn to our child and they are drawn to us, the Lord beckons to us and longs for us to draw near to him.

In our sorrow, we can either become focused on our overwhelming circumstances or we can direct our gaze on God to guide us through our overwhelming circumstances. Our outlook as we undergo fiery trials dramatically affects the outcomes after the fiery trial. Some people praise God in rough times for his faithfulness and goodness, but there are others who don't even know who he is or that his help is available to all who ask. I've had examples of both situations shared with me this week.

The first was a conversation with an acquaintance who recounted undergoing a succession of great losses and difficult trials. She said when situations are so painful, many people try to run rather than dealing with it but the only relief from her pain was to open up space for only her and God because God is the source of all comfort.

This mother of three spoke about the goodness of God and how amazing it is to be comforted by the God of the universe. When discussing her health issues which occurred after a major loss, she said, "I knew God "had it." Whether he healed me or healed me by taking me home, I knew he "had it" either way."

In contrast, just the day before this inspiring conversation, I had coffee with a friend I hadn't seen in quite some time. We had a great visit, but she also shared some sad news about a friend she used to work with. Years ago, he and his wife had a baby who was born with serious heart problems. I had worked with them in Intensive Care where their baby lived out her months and days before going to heaven. Sadly, the loss devastated their marriage. After they divorced, he turned to drugs and alcohol to cope with his pain, and he eventually lost his job. Tragically, the person my friend once knew was not the man he became which was a man without hope or comfort. My purpose in sharing this is not to discourage you but to encourage you to consider the message of Psalm 34:4 which says, "I sought the LORD and he answered me; he delivered me from all my fears." The good thing is that it's never too late to turn to God. God is a redeemer and a restorer and a deliverer.

Everyone goes through times of trouble and I am no exception. 2 Corinthians 1:3–5 encourages us to comfort others with the comfort we received from God. The Father of Compassion has delivered me from adversity and fear, and I desire the same for you as we each navigate our own heroic journey through this life.

Dear Lord,

I seek you and you answer me.
You quiet my fears and comfort my child
and I praise you.

In Jesus' name,
Amen

The righteous cry out, and the LORD hears them; he delivers them from all their troubles. The LORD is close to the brokenhearted and saves those who are crushed in spirit.
Psalm 34:17–18

Praise be to the God and Father of our Lord Jesus Christ, the Father of Compassion and the God of all comfort, who comforts us in all our troubles, so that we can comfort those in any trouble with the comfort we ourselves receive from God. For just as we share abundantly in the sufferings of Christ, so also our comfort abounds through Christ.

2 Corinthians 1:3–5

18

In Between

Nicki, a friend of mine, gave me a figurine of an angel. She is a talented music therapist, and we worked closely together at the hospital with our cardiology patients and their families. Nicki encountered some delay along her journey to motherhood and I, along with our friends, shared love and encouragement which we all need when our heart is aching.

When the time came for me to happily host her baby shower, Nicki arrived with a gift and a card. I unwrapped an angel of faith figurine accompanied with the words to Hebrews 11:1 which says, "Faith is being sure of what you hope for and certain of what you do not see." Nicki thanked me and told me I helped her to "not lose faith." Hard times are exhausting but friends make it better, especially when those friends point you towards Jesus who is the author and perfecter of our faith as Hebrews 12:2 describes.

I think of faith as faith that can be accessed "now." It is a focus on the present moment and a decision to push through doubt and discomfort.

It is a willingness to take a deep breath and say a quick "help me" prayer as well as a receptiveness to recognizing God's goodness as it is revealed in God's way and time. It is the leap of faith that carries you from one moment to another, one breath at a time.

In exercise class, my Barre3 instructor says that the work is done "in between." In between is where strength and growth develop; it's where all the hard work is done.

The Old Testament documents the story of the beautiful and brave Esther who was willing to submit her life for God's purposes.

The "in between" for Esther is where she went from being a young, orphaned girl being raised by her cousin to becoming Queen Esther married to a king. Esther was promoted to a position which held great risk for her, but she chose to have "now faith," and she succeeded in saving the Jewish people while the powerful enemy who had plotted against them was put to death.

In Esther 4, Esther's cousin Mordecai persuades her to risk her life and speak up on behalf of her Jewish people, asking her, "And who knows but that you have come to your royal position for such a time as this?" She was brought "this far" not to simply remain where she was, but to go further. It is the same for us.

The in between is where Nicki chose to "not lose faith." God's delays are not God's denials. Nicki and her husband moved beyond a place of pain and into new purpose and pursuits. They moved into the joy and challenge of parenthood and Nicki left hospital work for the flexibility of private practice.

2 Corinthians 5:7 says, "For we walk by faith, not by sight." The physical and the spiritual are equally real, but we can only see one realm with our physical eyes. The other is spiritually discerned.

Walking by faith happens when we choose to have faith in the moment of now, choosing to believe that God has the answers for our today and tomorrows.

Like Esther and Nicki, we've all faced situations that threatened to overwhelm us where we can't see beyond the great troubles looming before us. But that's not the end of the story. God knows all the storylines and the cast of characters involved. He knows the motives and hearts of men and women and nothing is hidden from him. God simply asks for us to trust him in the moment. His presence is near.

Our past, present, and future is in our Lord's steady hands. While we're here, in between the chapters of birth and Heaven, he beckons us to run with perseverance the race marked out for us. Our race is personal, and everyone is running their own race at their own pace. May we encourage others and be encouraged. Let's cheer each other on, especially when the terrain is rough.

Dear Lord,

Help me to have the faith now to move beyond what I can see or feel. Let me not grow weary and lose heart. Strengthen me to walk by faith and fix my eyes on Jesus, the author and perfecter of my faith.

In Jesus' name,
Amen

Now faith is being sure of what we hope for and certain of what we do not see. This is what the ancients were commended for. By faith we understand that the universe was formed at God's command, so that what is seen was not made out of what was visible.

Hebrews 11:1–3

Therefore, since we are surrounded by such a great cloud of witnesses, let us throw off everything that hinders and the sin that so easily entangles, and let us run with perseverance the race marked out for us. Let us fix our eyes on Jesus, the author and perfecter of our faith, who for the joy set before him endured the cross, scorning its shame, and sat down at the right hand of the throne of God. Consider him who endured such opposition from sinful men, so that you will not grow weary and lose heart.

Hebrew 12:1–3

19

Guideposts

By guest author, Meredith Adams

Our son was born with a serious congenital heart defect that had not been diagnosed before birth. The days and weeks immediately following his entrance into this world tested our previous reality and caused us to grow in our faith by leaps and bounds.

We were told he had a "difficult physiology" and the prognosis was not good. He had maybe a few weeks to live, no more than six months.

Having been raised in a Christian household, prayer was, of course, our response to the challenge. However, I lacked the belief that BIG miracles actually happened in this day and age. Irritated with family members who maintained a positive outlook, obviously not understanding the gravity of our situation, I snapped, "Miracles of this proportion only happened in biblical times. Or in the very rare occasions that you read about in Guideposts Magazine."

In that moment, I was so broken I could scarcely believe that I was special enough to God that a miracle of needed proportion could be ours. Over the next eighteen months, we were blown away by God's love.

He took that faith as small as a mustard seed and used our son to show us and everyone around us, the depth of his love. We witnessed countless miracles of epic proportion—we only needed to open our eyes and believe.

Dear Lord,

Your love is glorious! Please open our eyes to the understanding of your power and grace.

In Jesus' name,
Amen

If you believe you will see the Glory of the Lord.
John 11:40

With God, all things are possible.
Matthew 19:26

words of advice:

1. Find something positive in every day and write it down. Find joy in the smallest of things.

2. Don't be afraid to speak up, or to ask questions. You are your child's champion and advocate and your voice is important.

3. Find normalcy in an abnormal situation— participate in your child's care. Eat dinner off of real plates. Form friendships with those around you.

4. Find what you need to take care of you. Maybe it's crying in the shower. Maybe it's sitting in a sunbeam. Keep trying until you find your thing.

5. Accept help. Don't worry about pride, just open the door and allow yourself to be loved.

Meredith Adams is the mother of three beautiful children—one in Heaven and two on earth. She and her husband George are grateful for the friendships, deepening of faith and the gift of perspective they received during the year and a half they lived their life within sacred space at Nationwide Children's Hospital.

20

Oxygen Mask

By guest author, Tina Cole

My husband and I tried for eight years to become parents. I prayed every night for God to send me this precious gift. After several miscarriages, I questioned God's plan. I asked, "Am I worthy?"

I thought my prayers were faithful. I could not understand why my desire for a child was so strong, yet I was unable to carry one. I knew he was listening and I knew he had placed this desire in my heart. I asked for guidance and direction but I wasn't patient. It was not my time, and I eventually asked God to take the desire from my heart.

Around the time of one of my last miscarriages, I had dinner with a friend. We talked about my situation, and I felt a little better. She sent me a card the following week with Jeremiah 29:11, "For I know the plans I have for you," declares the LORD, "plans to prosper you and not to harm you, plans to give you hope and a future."

This brought me to my knees. My plans were not his plans. I was praying for my plans. This changed my prayers. I thanked him for what he had already given me. I thanked him for my husband, for my home, my health, my family, my job, my relationship with him. I thanked him for his plans for me in the moment. I had to be present and thankful for what I already had.

I had to put on my oxygen mask of faith and acknowledge that I needed to breathe it in to be able to function and go about my life. If you have ever flown on an airplane, then you have received this advice also. You must put on your own oxygen mask first and be aware of your surroundings before leaping to the next chapter. This lesson is critical and applies to so many areas of life.

Now, as a busy mother of five when I find myself eating dinner over a sink of dirty dishes at nine p.m. after the kids have been bathed and put to bed. Or the days I don't remember if I've used the bathroom or had a drink of water. I scold myself for not putting on my mask and taking better care of my needs now. Being a parent is exhausting but also a privilege and I certainly am thankful for the opportunity.

Dear Lord,

Your plan prospers me and gives me hope.
I am a happy mother of children and I praise you,
Lord.

In Jesus' name,
Amen

"For I know the plans I have for you," declares
the LORD, "plans to prosper you and not to harm
you, plans to give you hope and a future. Then
you will call upon me and come and pray to me,
and I will listen to you. You will seek me and find
me when you seek me with all your heart."
Jeremiah 29:11–13

He settles the barren woman in her home as a
happy mother of children. Praise the LORD.
Psalm 113:9

words of advice:

1. Drink water and remember to eat food, even snacks, to help you with strength and clarity.

2. Take a break from the bedside to change your scenery and clear your mind. You need time away from your child to be able to have your own thoughts and feelings and release your emotions.

3. Don't be afraid to advocate or share information that may help you or your child. Different people have different perspectives and ongoing communication is important.

4. Identify a contact person, someone you trust, to communicate and provide updates to others. This helps you focus on the priority of taking care of your child and diminishes the distraction and burden of retelling the same information.

5. Accept help, no matter how small or insignificant it may seem. People often want to help but don't know how to, so help direct them. Accept assistance in coordinating care for other children or pets. Be honest in sharing requests that would help or comfort maybe a new book to read to your child or a journal or magazines for you. Children can make cards or artwork for the patient's room or send personalized patient cards through the hospital's website.

Tina Cole is a Clinical Social Worker at Nationwide Children's Hospital with specialization in working with hospitalized children and their families. Tina and her husband Tracy have five children.

21

Psalm 9–1–1

Psalm 91 is a well-known Psalm about God's protection during times of danger. I refer to it as Psalm 9–1–1 because it seems relevant and helpful in any situation, especially when there is a sense of urgency involved. I've also heard this Psalm is often prayed by and for soldiers and troops in the military for their safety and protection.

This Psalm assures us of God's great promises to us such as his love for us, his provision to guard us and the promise of long life and salvation. Verse 1 says, "He who dwells in the shelter of the Most High will rest in the shadow of the Almighty." Verse 4 says, "He will cover you with his feathers, and under his wings you will find refuge." The visual that comes to mind is that of a mother bird protecting her baby birds in the warmth of her wings.

Psalm 91 acknowledges that very real dangers and threats exist and verse 7 says that many will fall, but it also says, "but it will not come near you." Psalm 91:14 says, "Because he loves me," says the LORD, "I will rescue him."

There are some specific times I know of where I was protected from the threat of real danger, but I'm sure we (and our family) are protected far more than we realize. For instance, a nurse friend took a walk with her two children one day when her son suddenly ran toward the street. Before my friend could respond, her daughter saw an angel push her brother safely from the edge of the street and away from an oncoming car.

God not only wants us close to him for safety but also for peace of mind and freedom from fear. Psalm 91:4 tells us that God's faithfulness is our shield and rampart and the following verse says, "You will not fear the terror of night." God wants to shield our minds from fear.

Hebrews 4:12 says, "For the word of God is living and active." God's word actively provides revelation. Proverbs 2:6 says, "For the LORD gives wisdom, and from his mouth come knowledge and understanding." Psalm 91 tells us that through God's faithfulness to us, when we stay as close as a shadow to him, he will give us wisdom and knowledge and understanding and he will guard us in all of our ways.

Dear Lord,

You are my refuge and my fortress,
and I trust in you.

In Jesus' name,
Amen

Psalm 91

He who dwells in the shelter of the Most High
will rest in the shadow of the Almighty.

I will say of the LORD, "He is my refuge and my
fortress, my God, in whom I trust."

Surely he will save you with his feathers, and
under his wings you will find refuge; his
faithfulness will be your shield and rampart.

You will not fear the terror of night, nor the arrow that flies by day,

nor the pestilence that stalks in the darkness, nor the plague that destroys at midday.

A thousand may fall at your side ten thousand at your right hand, but it will not come near you.

You will only observe with your eyes and see the punishment of the wicked.

If you make the Most High your dwelling— even the LORD, who is my refuge— then no harm will befall you, no disaster will come near your tent.

For he will command his angels concerning you to guard you in all your ways;

they will lift you up in their hands, so that you will not strike your foot against a stone,

You will tread upon the lion and the cobra; you will trample the great lion and the serpent.

"Because he loves me," says the LORD, "I will rescue him; I will protect him, for he acknowledges my name.

He will call upon me, and I will answer him; I will be with him in trouble, I will deliver him and honor him.

With long life will I satisfy him and show him my salvation."

Psalm 91:1–16

-22-

Think About It

Here's a question for you: how's your thought life? It's something to think about. I have definitely learned I need to pay attention to mine. Our minds are powerful and our thoughts shape who we are and direct our words and actions. Jeremiah 17:9 says, "The heart is deceitful above all things and beyond cure. Who can understand it?" We are told to guard our heart above all else in Proverbs 4:23 because it is the wellspring of life.

God's thoughts and ways are higher than our thoughts and ways. The Old Testament prophet Gideon had to change his thinking to match what God said about him. We need to do the same.

God's calling to Gideon as a military leader to the Israelites starts in the book of Judges beginning in chapter 6. To set the scene, the evil Midianites invaded the land of the Israelites, and the Israelites fled to the wilderness. A man named Gideon was threshing wheat in a winepress to keep it from the Midianites when the angel of the

LORD appeared to him. The angel said to Gideon, "The LORD is with you, mighty warrior."

Just let those powerful words sink in. "The LORD is with you, mighty warrior." You can read about Gideon in Judges 6–8, but he initially responded to the call with questioning and excuses about how he wasn't the man for the job. He cited that his clan was the weakest and he was the youngest and least in his family. God answered Gideon that he was sending him and he would be with him.

Gideon trusted God and an entire people were saved because of it. God chose Gideon and his army and then lead them to victory in an unlikely battle strategy. Gideon was a valiant warrior, and God calls us the same.

Gideon's thinking changed in response to God's word. Philippians 3:19 says, "Their mind is on earthly things. But our citizenship is in heaven." Gideon was thinking about earthly things until God's word transformed his thinking so he could understand heavenly things.

We are told what to think about and what to do, and they are described in Philippians 4:8–9. We are to think about excellent and lovely things. And the God of peace will be with us as we put into practice things we have learned from the Lord.

God uses the unlikely for his purposes. We are mighty warriors and the Lord is with us.

Dear Lord,

Help me to think about things that are excellent or praiseworthy for my citizenship is in heaven.

In Jesus' name,
Amen

Their mind is on earthly things. But our citizenship is in heaven.
> Philippians 3:19

Finally, brothers, whatever is true, whatever is noble, whatever is right, whatever is pure, whatever is lovely, whatever is admirable—if anything is excellent or praiseworthy—think about such things. Whatever you have learned or received or heard from me, or seen in me—put it into practice. And the God of peace will be with you.

Philippians 4:8–9

23

Expect Miracles

There are so many interesting aspects about the story of Gideon. Looking again at the conversation between the angel of the LORD and Gideon in Judges 6, Gideon asks, "if the LORD is with us, why has all this happened to us? Where are all his wonders that our fathers told us about when they said, 'Did not the LORD bring us up out of Egypt?' But now the LORD has abandoned us and put us into the hand of Midian."

Gideon was raised with the knowledge of a Sovereign God who delivered his people from captivity to the Promised Land. With God's permission, Gideon tested the Lord and then Judges 6:22 documents when Gideon realized the holy encounter for what it was and exclaimed, "Ah, Sovereign LORD! I have seen the angel of the LORD face to face!"

With enemies occupying his land, rescue could only come about through the means of a miracle. The Midianites greatly outnumbered the Israelites, yet the Lord told Gideon that he had too many men in his army because he did not want the Israelites to boast in their own strength. God told Gideon to send home those who trembled in fear. Judges 7:3 documents, "so twenty-two thousand men left, while ten thousand remained."

Then the Lord told Gideon there were still too many men and instructed him to take them down to the water. In Judges 7:5, the Lord told him, "Separate those who lap the water with their tongues like a dog from those who kneel down to drink." Three hundred men lapped with their hands to their mouths while the rest got down on their knees to drink. Three hundred men were chosen from ten thousand because of how they drank water. The Lord's ways are not our ways and his way for us is through faith and not fear.

The Lord lead Gideon and his army to victory using only trumpets, empty jars, lit torches and their voices to shout, "For the LORD and for Gideon."

There's no set formula how God performs miracles. He can do it any way he wants. He heals and delivers specifically. I wonder how many people miss miracles because they aren't expecting one? Jeremiah 32:27 says, "I am the LORD, the God of all mankind. Is anything too hard for me?" Psalm 46:10 says, "Be still, and know that I am God; I will be exalted among the nations, I will be exalted in the earth." God can be exalted through the miracles in our lives. Not only can we be healed, delivered and saved, but others will be affected and blessed by the miracles in our lives and God will be exalted.

Gideon was raised hearing about the wonders of the LORD. In the increasingly fearful culture in which we live, are we raising our children to hear the wonders of the Lord? Can we focus not on the battles, but on the deliverance; and not on the illness but on the healing?

When we go through the really hard things of this world, how do we respond and how do we teach our children to respond? 1 Peter 4:12–13 says, "Do not be surprised at the painful trial you are suffering, as though something strange were happening to you. But rejoice that you participate in the sufferings of Christ, so that you may be overjoyed when his glory is revealed."

Psalm 98:1 says, "Sing to the LORD a new song, for he has done marvelous things." May our expectation be from the Lord and may he be exalted through the marvelous things he does.

I have a friend who went through a very serious illness with a poor prognosis a few years ago. She said she felt "told what to do" all throughout that extremely difficult time. While she was still in the hospital after emergency surgery, she and her husband made the decision to move their family across the country to a warmer climate and a more active lifestyle. After they had relocated, she learned her new physician was actually a leading authority in treating her specific diagnosis and he, like other doctors, were amazed at her incredible recovery which exceeded anyone's estimation. Nothing is too hard for the Lord.

Dear Lord,

You perform miracles that cannot be counted, and I sing a new song for you do marvelous things.

In Jesus' name,
Amen

Then the word of the LORD came to Jeremiah: "I am the LORD, the God of all mankind. Is anything too hard for me?

Jeremiah 32:27

"But if it were I, I would appeal to God; I would lay my cause before him. He performs wonders that cannot be fathomed, miracles that cannot be counted.

Job 5:8–9

24

The Drop Off

The movie titled Finding Nemo has always been one of our family favorites, and it was the first movie that our daughter, Audrey, really watched and loved. She saw it at her cousin's house when she was two years old during a living room camp out. I occasionally glanced at her in the next room, snuggled next to her older cousin and belly laughing out loud at funny parts, including Dory's singing "just keep swimming."

The movie has wide appeal and accesses a range of emotions. Nemo is a clownfish who is raised by his overprotective father, Marlin. When Nemo starts school, his father struggles with releasing the care of his son to another, Nemo's teacher, because he is concerned for his safety.

A crisis occurs which prompts Marlin to journey across the ocean, far from his home and way beyond his comfort zone. He befriends a blue tang fish named Dory. Together they encounter danger and adventure as they grow in perspective and character. The dynamic of tension between parent and child is seen in the struggle between independence and supervision. Sometimes it's difficult to know how to foster independence with children in an unsafe world. Many decisions need to be made along the way.

We vacationed in Bermuda this summer and chose accommodations with teenagers in mind. Audrey's friend Elena joined us, and the four of us had a great time. Teenagers need fun, activity, choices, and independence and we parents need perimeters and peace of mind. We stayed at a family run oceanfront resort with several restaurants, water sports and a small, private beach with beautiful aqua clear water. The beach had a shallow waterfront and was situated on a large sand bar which extended far into the ocean. It was like swimming in an aquarium. We floated on rafts for hours in the clear blue water watching fish swimming around us. There were two large floating wood platforms a distance away from shore that people swam to and rested on.

One day we went on a jet ski tour in the morning. Afterward we returned to the resort for lunch where Audrey and Elena discussed their plans to go snorkeling. There were big rocks and a cove outside the beach area they could explore, and they could swim and snorkel out to the floating wood platforms.

After lunch, they headed to the water sports center, and I went back to the room for about a half hour before meeting Ed at the beach. Our room was located up on a hill, and I could clearly see down to the beach and the water. Two people were floating on rafts and two boats anchored in the water, but I didn't see Audrey and Elena. I made my way down to the beach and asked Ed where the girls were. He answered that he hadn't seen them but had been looking for them. He guessed they were snorkeling near some large rocks nearby.

When I heard Ed hadn't seen them, panic set in immediately. We each grabbed a raft and swam in different directions, signaling to one another. I swam out to one of the boats where kids were playing in the water with their parents on board and learned they hadn't seen any snorkelers. I signaled to Ed to swim back to the beach, and by the time we reached the shore, the girls had been missing for more than an hour.

I ran back up to our room in case we had somehow missed them and Ed headed to the water sports center to get a kayak. He eventually found the girls snorkeling behind a boat at the reef.

From our parental perspective, we were concerned we couldn't find them in clear and open water. Also concerning is that they chose to snorkel hidden behind and close to a boat of strangers.

From their teen perspective, they were doing exactly what they had been told to do by the water sports dude. They had been directed to the reef when they rented the snorkeling equipment, and they were doing just that when they looked up and saw Ed coming at them speedily in a kayak with a look of determination on his face. They were not expecting to see him while they were exploring the undersea world. They were upset and confused to be directed back to the hotel room for a little while so our heart rhythms could return back to normal.

During the time Audrey and Elena were snorkeling in an unknown location, Elena's parents, good friends of ours, texted me and asked how we were all doing. While we vacationed in Bermuda, they visited California vineyards, and we shared photos and texts throughout the day.

At the moment I received their text, I happened to be at the beach hyperventilating and praying.

With shaking hands, I texted about our fun day jet skiing in the morning, lunch on the patio by the pool and how the girls were snorkeling while Ed and I were at the beach. I knew there was no need to alarm them. My fear was serious but so is my faith. I know God knows the plans he has for these precious girls and they are plans for good. That is the promise of Jeremiah 29:11 and it was what I focused on even with an anxious body and mind because I know the Lord who reigns and he is over all.

After some recovery time, we all calmed down, and the girls forgave us. They thought our reaction was extreme, but they could understand our fear. We moved on with our day, but we all felt the impact of the stress it had brought.

By the next day, I could see some humor in the situation. Ed and I sometimes ate breakfast by ourselves because the girls preferred to sleep in and have a later breakfast.

When Audrey and Elena joined me at the beach after their breakfast, I apologized for the misunderstanding, and they said they could understand our concern. I told them I'd been giggling that morning to myself how I reacted just like Marlin did when he learned Nemo and his school of fish were going to the drop off.

I imitated Marlin's hysterical voice, "The drop off! They're going to the drop off!? What? Are you insane? Why don't we just fry them up now and serve them with chips?!" I'm glad we were able to laugh about it together.

What the Lord revealed to me through this experience is how he can keep us safe under the shelter of his wings like Psalm 91 proclaims. Just as Audrey and Elena were hidden in the plain sight of clear and open water, God can protect us, so we are also hidden in plain sight.

The world is full of real dangers, and so is the ocean. But the Maker of Heaven and Earth also makes a place of safety for us, and that place of safety is under the shelter of his wings.

And this is something I need to remember always. Especially in the Fall when we take Audrey to college for the first time, the ultimate of "drop off" experiences.

Things change and life goes on. Children become teenagers and teenagers become adults. We need to appreciate each day while we just keep swimming into the full capacity that God has for us. And, like Dory, that's something to sing about.

Dear Lord,

When anxiety was great within me, your consolation brought joy to my soul. Help me to overcome fear and find refuge in you under the cover of your wings.

 In Jesus' name,
Amen

He will cover you with his feathers, and under his wings you will find refuge; his faithfulness will be your shield and rampart.

Psalm 91:4

When anxiety was great within me, your consolation brought joy to my soul.

Psalm 94:19

25

Rescue

This summer, we vacationed in beautiful and welcoming Bermuda. It was a wonderful trip, and we were accompanied by Audrey and her friend Elena. We enjoyed beautiful weather and some special moments, but I also enjoyed the sense of community of both the resort and the island.

One morning while Ed and I were having breakfast on a terrace overlooking the pool, we watched several sparrows chirping and gathering on the pool decks. One of the sparrows sat on the edge of the pool, then fell in. The other sparrows gathered around it, hopping and chirping, obviously in distress as the sparrow in the water tried unsuccessfully to get out.

Two sisters, who looked to be four and six years old, rushed over and gently tried to scoop the bird out of the water. The older sister continued in her rescue efforts while the younger girl hurried away and returned quickly with her dad who jogged behind her carrying a scuba fin. He gently put the fin in the water and lifted the bird safely to land. They sat and watched the bird to see if it was okay. Then the sisters got some muffin crumbs and began to feed it. The bird appeared to be fine. His bird community gathered around him and they flittered away.

A little later, the sisters and their mom settled into the lounge chairs next to mine at the beach. I told them we had watched them rescue the bird from the pool and I thanked them for their courage and caring. Their Mom answered saying she was surprised by their reaction and she is so pleased they are such good girls.

Proverbs 22:6 says, "Train a child in the way he should go, and when he is old he will not depart from it." Children raised with love and compassion and respect for life will live out these values.

In this dark world, despite blaring and bleak headlines, I choose to remember the many competent and compassionate people I know, who live with purpose and intention. These are people who know great troubles exist, and they are people who have gone through great troubles themselves, yet they chose to participate in treating the problem or easing the pain. These are hopeful, not hopeless people. They are brave, imperfect people reflecting light in the fallen world around them.

The fallen bird, the flock of distressed sparrows and the attentive rescuers remind me of scenes so often played out in the trauma room. In a trauma alert, attention is focused on the patient, with the patient's distressed family unable to help their child on their own and a trauma team surrounding the patient's bed, the capable rescuers. The rescuers assess and intervene. They console the patient, speaking words of encouragement and explanation while performing medical care and intervention.

One of the child life specialists said that hospital work is hard work and not only is it hard work, but it is heart work. A life of significance comes from having a life of purpose. It is compassion and purpose that prompted two young girls to save a drowning bird. It is with compassion and purpose that we are also called to use our life which has been given as a gift to us.

Sometimes we are the fallen bird, sometimes we are the distressed onlooker, and sometimes we are the rescuer. But in all times and all circumstances, we can call to our Heavenly Father, who will rush in with a scuba fin or

153

whatever means necessary to lift us out of a dire place.

Dear Lord,

You are the ultimate rescuer. Thank you for sending your son, our Lord and Savior Jesus Christ, to die on the cross for our sins so we may live eternally with you. May I live with compassion and purpose, reflecting your light in a hurting world.

In Jesus' name,
Amen

Though I have fallen, I will rise. Though I sit in darkness, The LORD will be my light.
Micah 7:8

Therefore I tell you, do not worry about your life, what you will eat or drink; or about your body, what you will wear. Is not life more important than food, and the body more important than clothes? Look at the birds of the air; they do not sow or reap or store away in barns, and yet your heavenly Father feeds them. Are you not much more valuable than they? Who of you by worrying can add a single hour to this life?

Matthew 6:25

26

Bear Hunt

At the hospital, in music group we often sang the Bear Hunt song, "We're going on a bear hunt, I'm not afraid!"

When going on a bear hunt or traveling through some other dangerous episode or adventure, it helps to acquire a mindset of perseverance. Most challenges require time and space to work themselves out and details and adjustment typically occur through a series of events or phases.

One family I worked with said that wading through grief was like going on a bear hunt. As intense and painful as their grief was, they couldn't go over it, they couldn't go under it and they couldn't go around it. They could only go through it.

Going through it, is unfortunately, the only way to get to the other side. I currently have a friend who is going through something hard. She is a ninja mom from my prayer group who just received a new diagnosis. Her recent days have been busy with physician and procedural appointments as she prepares for upcoming surgery and treatment plans beyond that. It is overwhelming to receive news like that, regardless of your level of faith and hers is strong.

She is mentally preparing herself for the days and months ahead and what it will require of her. She doesn't want to go through what she has to go through but she says the Lord is with her and telling her to praise him. Psalm 34:19 says, "A righteous man may have many troubles, but the LORD delivers him from them all."

I take comfort in the words of Isaiah 43 which says, "*When you...*" Isaiah 43 says, "Fear not, for I have redeemed you; I have summoned you by name; you are mine." It continues with, "*When you* pass through the waters" and "*When you* pass through the fire." It doesn't mention, "*If you pass*" but instead it says, "*When you pass.*"

The prophet Isaiah assures us that because the Lord calls us by name and because we are his, *when* we go through rivers, they will not sweep us away and *when* we walk through the fire, the flames won't set us ablaze and we will not be burned.

The Bible is full of examples of overcomers who went through very challenging times before they were delivered. Jesus, Moses, Noah, David, Esther, Daniel and Gideon come easily to mind but there are so many others. They, like me, have passed through the waters without being swept away and have walked through fire without being burned.

The Lord has summoned us each by name. He says to us, "You are mine." We live among many problems in this broken world but we are told what to do about it in Psalm 141:8. We are told to fix our eyes on our Sovereign Lord for safety and protection from death. Psalm 46:1 says, "God is our refuge and strength, an ever-present help in trouble."

The thing to remember about a bear hunt is to not be afraid. God's not afraid of bears (he made them) and reverence for our Holy Lord is our strength and peace and joy. He is our God and our guide as we pass through exciting new adventures and when we travel through bear country or lands of trial. We can exchange our fear for faith and follow our guide for he knows the way because he is the way.

Dear Lord,

Help me to fix my eyes on you for you are my refuge.

In Jesus' name,
Amen

But my eyes are fixed on you, O Sovereign LORD; in you I take refuge—do not give me over to death.

Psalm 141:8

"Fear not, for I have redeemed you; I have summoned you by name; you are mine. When you pass through the waters, I will be with you; and when you pass through the rivers, they will not sweep over you. When you walk through the fire, you will not be burned; the flames will not set you ablaze. For I am the LORD, your God, the Holy One of Israel, your Savior.

Isaiah 43:1–3

-27-

Say Anything

There are cornfields at the end of our road which belong to a neighboring university. When we moved here many years ago, I couldn't have anticipated how significant those fields would become to me.

As a family, we've taken many walks and bike rides on the paved path through the cornfields which lead to a large park and bike paths. Around the cornfields are wide dirt roads which lead to both cleared and wooded areas that are great for exploring with our dogs.

Audrey became an expert tree climber in the trees that line the fields. She has a favorite tree which is especially good for climbing. For a sweet season in time, she asked us to take her there every night, which we did, our dog at our side.

Now that she's a busy teenager with things to do and people to see, Ed and I walk together again like before we were three.

One of my sisters lives a few houses down, and Dana and I frequent the fields with our collective four dogs between us. We've had a lot of great talks along the way. We've walked with our kids from strollers to skateboards and we've walked many dogs. We've walked those paths through illnesses and we now walk them in good health.

But many of my trips to and through the fields occur during the day with only the dogs. Audrey collects stickers on her water bottle, and one of them says "go outside more" which is exactly what I've done in recent years. Spending more time in nature has awakened my senses in a greater way to the beauty around me. It has also cultivated my ability to hear the voice of God in a clearer way.

There have been some changes recently with big things to think about, and the fields are a good place for reflection. The fields reflect the changing seasons. The corn stalks were cut down late this year, and the fields are bare and exposed again. The swirling energy of the Fall winds can be felt as they blow the leaves from their trees. Next season will bring a blanket of snow.

The Bible says a lot about the times and seasons. One of the lessons gleaned while observing how tall the stalks of corn had grown was a lesson in blessing distribution. Sometimes I shop at TJ

Maxx and buy "past season" clothing. What was revealed is that there is no problem with "past season" clothing but there *is* a problem with "past season" blessings. God has reserved blessings for *every s*eason. While I know past and present blessings, I don't know what future blessings God has for me. But they exist and I'm asked to be flexible and open to receiving them.

James 2:17 says that every good and perfect gift is from above, coming down from the Father of the heavenly lights. In Matthew 7:11, Jesus talks about how parents give good gifts to their children and how much more our Father in Heaven gives good gifts to those who ask him. God is a gift giver. God's revelation and guidance are among his gifts.

Jesus spoke in parables and in Matthew 13:10–11, his disciples asked him why. Jesus answered, "The knowledge of the secrets of the kingdom of heaven has been given to you, but not to them."

So, Jesus is saying that there are secrets of the kingdom of heaven and he wants to give us the knowledge of those secrets. But the thing is, not everyone is going to be able to understand them. The scripture goes on to explain that some people will see and hear what Jesus is saying, but they will not be able to perceive or understand the message of what Jesus says. The people who *do* understand what Jesus says have the spiritual eyes to see and spiritual ears to hear his truth with a heart to understand the meaning.

By outward appearances, it looks like I'm a woman walking my dogs. But beyond that, I am learning and understanding deep and hidden things that are being revealed which are secrets of the kingdom of heaven. It's been a really good thing for me to go outside more. And in the process, I've given God more access to the inside of me. But apparently not enough access.

A few weeks ago, the dogs and I were at the field on a warm sunny day when the words "say anything" were given to my heart. I didn't know what that meant. I thought and prayed about it throughout the day until I understood the meaning. Turns out, the message is about trust. Specifically, about trusting God with all my heart.

God revealed my heart is still guarded. He wants me to work towards a higher level of trust with the freedom for me to tell him, "say anything." My initial reaction was thinking how that was crazy talk. My mind immediately recalled the

166

knowledge a few years ago that God was leading me out of my extensive child life work at the hospital for a purpose I couldn't yet understand and that it was going to be a "promotion." But I certainly did not anticipate the exit strategy would include overcoming disease in the interim. Yet he healed me and used it for his purposes. God proved himself mighty on my behalf yet once again. And God doesn't just give life, he gives abundant life, so he's asking me to broaden my thinking to let him say anything he wants to me.

On and off the cornfields, I encourage my dogs, Rowen and Houston, to listen and respond. I call to them with affection. I know God does the same with me.

I'm working on praying "say anything," even though God and I both know that I don't really mean it yet. But I'm going to fake it until I make it because you've got to start somewhere.

Dear Lord,

Say anything. For you know everything.

In Jesus' name,
Amen

The knowledge of the secrets of the kingdom of heaven has been given to you, but not to them.
>> Matthew 13:11

He changes times and seasons; he sets up kings and deposes them. He gives wisdom to the wise and knowledge to the discerning. He reveals deep and hidden things, he knows what lies in darkness and light dwells with him.
>> Daniel 2:21–22

28

Words Have Power

One morning before work, I randomly turned on the TV and saw a few minutes of a woman's interview regarding being healed from a terminal illness. She credited God for her healing and said she recovered by taking a "dose" of scripture three times a day just as some people take medication three times a day. She said reading scripture aloud activated healing and faith, making her stronger in body and mind. Her doctors called her recovery a miracle. I only watched a few minutes, but it was powerful.

I now have a deeper understanding of what she was talking about. There can be a lot of blame and negativity surrounding illness and injury and all the issues relating to it. Crisis can trigger deep emotions, and it often doesn't bring out the best in any of us. Wading through the complexity of illness can also be physically and emotionally exhausting.

In college, I learned the stress of hospitalization can interfere with parent's comprehension and understanding of medical information being relayed. I've seen that with parents and I've experienced it myself. I'm an advocate of writing things down, asking questions and later assessing the information.

Not only is the information being relayed important but the delivery of the information is also important. At the hospital, we use developmentally appropriate and non-threatening language when talking with patients. We adapt our communication and intervention based on each individual situation.

One day at work my friend Denny, an ER nurse and EMT, told me about a recent situation he had working at the firehouse. He was called to the scene of an accident where a ten-year-old boy had been hit by a car. Denny and the other EMT put him on a backboard and stabilized his neck to transport him to the hospital safely. Pain and fear are good reasons to cry, and this boy was crying. In the ambulance, the other EMT sat near the patient's head while Denny was positioned near his feet.

The other EMT, trying to comfort the boy said, "Hey, kid! Shut up! You're going to be okay." Denny glanced at the EMT and said, "Trade me places."

172

Denny knew he could convey encouragement and understanding more effectively to the hurt and scared boy while realizing the EMT had seen far more critical situations and was trying to assure the child he would be fine.

Denny also knows it's very important whose voice you listen to. What and who you listen to directs your thoughts and actions. Our mind influences our heart, and our heart influences our tongue. Proverbs 18:21 says, "The tongue has the power of life and death, and those who love it will eat its fruit." Words have power. We can speak either life or death, and they will produce different results over our health and well-being. We need to monitor our self-talk as well.

A friend's high school football coach told him that the mind gives out before the body, so it is important to pay attention to your thoughts. Proverbs 15:3 explains the tongue that brings healing is a tree of life. It goes on to warn that a deceitful tongue crushes the spirit. Our words can bring healing or our words can crush our spirit. So what we say and how we say it is important. We need to be a friend to ourselves and to others.

My daughter struggled with earaches throughout the summer. I felt terrible for her. She had several doctor visits, an urgent care visit and multiple rounds of prescriptions but nothing completely treated it. After yet another trip to the doctor's office, she was referred to an ENT (Ear, Nose, and Throat) specialist but she couldn't be seen for several days, and she was in serious pain. After leaving the doctor's office after yet another visit, I decided to drive straight to children's hospital ER where she was admitted overnight for inner and outer ear infections and a ruptured eardrum.

I replayed in my mind what I could have done differently or sooner and then I just stopped myself from those thoughts. A lot of times, it's hard to know what to do, and as a child life specialist for so many years, I understand that. Parents and patients often blame themselves and that isn't helpful. We can speak encouragement or discouragement, life or death. Sometimes we need to be our own best friend and speak life and encouragement over our own lives and circumstances, reminding ourselves of God's promises.

Hebrews 4:12 describes the word of God as living and active and Isaiah 55:11 promises God's word

174

will not return void but accomplishes specific purposes which God desires. The healed woman on the TV interview knew that the Bible is full of scriptures about healing and abundant life. As she took her "doses" of scripture as medicine, the living and active word of God strengthened and healed her and God was glorified. Even the doctors knew her recovery was beyond what they could have imagined.

We can be instrumental in our own recovery and for those we love by speaking life, health, hope and restoration. And we can all use a friend like that.

Dear Lord,

Your Word is living and active. May my heart and mind be focused on you so that I can speak life and hope. Thank you that your word accomplishes the healing and purposes for which you send it. Align the desires of my heart to align with the desires of yours.

In Jesus' name,
Amen

For the word of God is living and active. Sharper than any double-edged sword, it penetrates even to dividing soul and spirit, joints and marrow, it judges the thoughts and attitudes of the heart.
Hebrews 4:12

So it is my word that goes out from my mouth; It will not return to me empty, but will accomplish what I desire and achieve the purpose for which I sent it.
Isaiah 55:11

29

Fun House

During my brother's college years, he worked as a musician at a popular amusement park, Cedar Point. The park has a large hotel with a private beach across the street from it, and our family has a long tradition of going to Cedar Point and staying at the hotel as a family. From strollers to rollercoasters, our children have grown up riding rides and making memories with their cousins. I'm sure they will continue to do the same in later years when they have children of their own.

I like roller coasters but I don't like the fun house. I used to brace myself and tensely walk through it just to get to the tube slides at the end. I eventually figured out that the slide part wasn't worth the stress of traveling through the fun house which I didn't find fun. I think my startle reflex is set a little higher than it should be and I try to tone it down, not trigger it.

My brother likes the fun house. I remember walking through the dark rooms with sensory overload, walking on a squishy floor surface through one area and next walking across a bridge in a room with spinning walls.

In college, during my brother's many trips through the fun house, he figured out that walking through the fun house was a lot like walking by faith. There are many voices and distractions but the key to walking through the fun house, he said, was to look straight ahead at one focal point at the end and then it's easy. All the noise and distractions are secondary and continue to go on around you, but the path is made clear once you know what direction to follow.

One year when my brother and sister-in-law went through the fun house with their kids, one of their kids was afraid. My brother spoke to his son, saying his name and assuring him he was right behind him. After my nephew heard his father's voice, he heard many other voices all calling his name in the dark from different places in the room, some of them very close to him. The fun house workers wore night vision goggles and were calling his name. My nephew stayed close to his father's comforting presence as they walked through the dark rooms until they exited into the light of the day.

There are times in life that remind me of that fun house, times when circumstances have been dark, confusing and weird. But going through these times have helped to direct my focus and refine my purpose to the things that really matter most. Distractions and voices and messages bombard our senses and are part of the chaos of life. Some of it we can turn off and some of it we can't.

Philippians 3:19–20 says, "Their mind is on earthly things. But our citizenship is in heaven. In John 17, Jesus explains how God sent him into the world and how he resided "in" the world but that he is not "of" the world. Jesus explains the same is true for us, that we are also sent into the world to be sanctified by the truth of the Word of God. John 17:15 shares Jesus' prayer for us which says, "My prayer is not that you take them out of the world but that you protect them from the evil one. They are not of the world, even as I am not of it."

I don't stay away from the amusement park, I navigate through it. God didn't choose to spare us from navigating through life with all its thrills and trials, but he is the one who sent us and guides us through it. And not only that, he entrusts us with our children so that we, like Jesus, pray for their protection from evil and for their lives to be sanctified by the truth of the word of God. Many around us are only focused on earthly things but we must not forget our citizenship is in heaven.

Many voices call our name, but only one will lead us to our heavenly home. Isaiah 31:21 instructs, "Whether you turn to the right or to the left, your ears will hear a voice behind you, saying, "This is the way; walk in it." It's a voice we know. It's God's voice who first sent us into the world and it's his voice who will welcome us home.

Dear Lord,

Guide me in this world for my citizenship is in heaven. Protect my family and I from evil and guide us in the fullness of your truth and purpose for our lives. In love and wisdom, you reign above the noise and chaos that attempt to distract me. Help me to stay focused on you and help me to teach my child the same.

In Jesus' name,
Amen

Let your eyes look straight ahead, fix your gaze directly before you. Make level paths for your feet and take only ways that are firm. Do not swerve to the right or the left; keep your foot from evil.

Proverbs 4:25–27

My prayer is not that you take them out of the world but that you protect them from the evil one. They are not of the world, even as I am not of it. Sanctify them by the truth; your word is truth. As you sent me into the world, I have sent them into the world. For them I sanctify myself, that they too may be truly sanctified.

John 17:15–19

30

Caretakers

In talking with a hospital chaplain one day, he shared about some of his clinical experiences and talked about his role comforting and encouraging patients, families, and staff. He said, "We're the agents of the day." Ephesians 2:10 says, "For we are God's workmanship, created in Christ Jesus to do good works, which God prepared in advance for us to do."

This chaplain was a businessman and a busy family man whose life was interrupted when he felt impressed to return to school to become a chaplain. Through the process, his faith was strengthened, his capacity for compassion grew, and he found even greater personal fulfillment than he had before.

Our main purpose, the reason why we're here, is to love God and love others. John 13:35 says that our love for one another demonstrates to all men that we are God's disciples. The Lord is full of compassion and perhaps we are most like him when we're taking care of others. God's supernatural love is transforming, it flows to us and through us.

At prayer group recently, after praying for specific issues affecting our teenagers and community, one of the mom's said, "We're the caretakers. We need to take care of this moment in time." Philippians 2:4 says, "Each of you should look not only to your own interests but also to the interests of others."

Our small group of busy women gathers to pray because we know how precious children and families are to the heart of God. Children are born small, weak and vulnerable, so I think God tries to let us know from the beginning that the job of parenting is way beyond our capabilities and that we're going to need his help.

Scripture tells us that children are a gift from God. Psalm 127:3 says children are a reward from him and James 1:17 says that every good and perfect gift is from the Father of heavenly Lights. In Jeremiah 1:5, it is written, "Before I formed you in the womb I knew you," referencing a relationship that precedes the womb.

Isaiah 54:13 says that children will be taught by the Lord and will have great peace.

Deuteronomy 6 instructs us to love the Lord and teach the commandments to our children and Proverbs 22:6 explains a child raised in the ways of the Lord will not turn away from those teachings when they are old.

Psalm 16:11 says, "You have made known to me the path of life; you will fill me with joy in your presence, with eternal pleasures at your right hand. This verse indicates the psalmist *became aware* of the path of life. God reveals knowledge and understanding he wants to be made known to us. Joy in God's presence and eternal pleasures existed before the psalmist's understanding, but then God *made known to him* the path of life.

Gideon was made known about the wonders of the LORD who had saved his people and brought them out of captivity. What I wonder about is this: how many children in today's culture know about the wonders of the Lord? My concern is that too many children are struggling and too few know God as the path of life. From my assessment, there are too many kids in crisis who are depleted physically, emotionally and spiritually and often, concerned parents who don't know how to help them.

Jesus said in Matthew 19:41, "Let the little children come to me, and do not hinder them, for the kingdom of heaven belongs to such as these." Children are hindered when they are not taught about God's love, and they are hindered when they are not prayed for. 2 Corinthians 4:18 instructs us to fix our eyes not on what is seen, which is temporary, but to focus on what is unseen, for it is eternal.

We're God's caretakers. All children are ours because all children are his. I implore you to seek God to open your eyes to the needs of children around you in whatever ways God leads you specifically. It may be as simple as praying for the local school or for a family in your neighborhood. Now is the time for us to be the agents of the day. In 2 Chronicles 7:14, God says, "If my people, who are called by my name, will humble themselves and pray and seek my face and turn from their wicked ways, then I will hear from heaven and will forgive their sin and will heal their land. Now my eyes will be open and my ears attentive to the prayers offered in this place." No matter who we are or what mistakes we've made, the Lord knows us and always wants us to turn to him in our brokenness to forgive us and heal us.

God's ways are higher than our ways and God is calling us to his higher ways. God's Word instructs us to live in harmony with one another and to conquer evil with good, but these things and other miracles can only be accomplished through God's power and transforming love.

So, it all starts with us. It begins with us calling to God and he will not only answer us, but he will tell us great and unsearchable things that we do not know. Jeremiah 33:6 says, "Nevertheless, I will bring health and healing to it; I will heal my people and let them enjoy abundant peace and security.

God's love changes us. We are known, loved, forgiven and cherished. Isaiah 61:9 says, "All who see them will acknowledge that they are a people the LORD has blessed."

We are God's unlikely army for this moment in time. Whether you are in a hospital room or elsewhere, God's truth and love is for you and it's for you to share with others in this hurting world.

May the Lord bless you and your family. May God's healing and abundant peace be with you always.

Dear Lord,

I lift up my hands to you for the life of my child and for all your children.

In Jesus' name,
Amen

Pour out your heart like water in the presence of the Lord. Lift up your hands to him for the lives of your children.
Lamentations 2:19

Jesus said, "Let the little children come to me, and do not hinder them, for the kingdom of heaven belongs to such as these."
Matthew 19:14